DIARY OF A TEAR - CUTTER

Title: DIARY OF A TEAR - CUTTER

by Stefanie Bennett
ISBN 9781877010194

DIARY OF A TEAR - CUTTER is a combined Cochon & Golden Hill publication

Copyright:
'The Golden Hill Paugussett Indian Nation'

This book is copyright. Apart from fair dealing for the purpose of private study, research or review as permitted under the Copyright Act, no part may be reproduced, stored in a retrieval system or transmitted in any other form without written permission.

In memory of Judith Rodriguez & those who've supported my work & words over the last few years. I thank you for the time you have given me.

Published by
Burringbah Books
PO Box 368
North Hobart
Tasmania 7002

Burringbah
Books

DIARY OF A TEAR - CUTTER

STEFANIE BENNETT

During "Love Minus Zero, No Limit"

Joan Baez

ACKNOWLEDGEMENTS

Some of the poems in this collection have been published by *Southerly Magazine, I Am Not A Silent Poet, Virgo Gray Press, Best New Poems (111.), The Lake Journal, Beyond The Rainbow Magazine, Prolific Press, The Mad Hatter's Review, The Foundation Of Australian Literary Studies, In Between Hangovers, UFO Gigolo, The Paterson Literary Review, Poems To Empower, Indiana Voice Journal, Three North Queensland Poets, Cave Press, Madness Muse Magazine, Shot Glass Journal, The Bijou Review, Maleny & District Community Publishing, Boston Poetry Magazine, Carcinogenic Poetry, Whisperings, Message In A Bottle, Record Magazine, Dead Snakes, Denesene Tampa Label, MAD Swirl, Dissident Voice Magazine, Chicago Reader, Project Agent Orange, NewVerse News, Open Mouse Poetry, Ecord, The Galway Review, Kind Of A Hurricane Press Anthology, Every Day Poems, Degenerative Literature, Plum Tree Tavern, Every Writer's Resource Magazine, The Pangolin Review, Bindweed Magazine, Your One Phone Call, Haggard And Halloo, VerseWrights, Eskimo Pie, Orbitt Nett, Scarlet Leaf Review, Illuminations Galerie, Poetry Pacific, Rasputin, High Coupe, The Poetry Zine LA, Wild & Woolley, Shadow Craft, Aust. Music Centre* - others.

Cover Photo: Tania Kavney

Back Cover: Stefanie Bennett

This publication is made possible by a gift and grant from - THE GOLDEN HILL INDIAN NATION at Trumbull, Connecticut, USA and in agreement with the author 2019.

CONTENTS

(Alison Croggon) Quote, Part One
Opus for Heart and Stone
(Dan Gerber) Quote
Wanted
Multiplication
Don't Cry My Children
A General Truth
Hearts That Die Young
The Cairn
Cutting The Chaff
Wings
Journal Entry
Mt. Etna and Horses of the Moon: a Song
for the Azure Cameo
I could Not Tell You (for Anna-Marie, aged 7)
Restitution
Heart
After 'Of Gods and Olives'
Athena Regrets
Now and Then
Miniature
For All Nuclear Scientists: The Killing & the Telling
The Hurt
Tower
Memento ... the Mountain of Suns
The Curse: Hamlet
The Devine Fem
Following the Ballad 'Gorbanevskaya'
The Brief
Scope and Validation
Geneva's Sweet Tweets

Iris Oracle
Earth, Wind, Fire
Home Grown
Guest
Baggage
Passage - Moscow 1915
My Grandfather's Violin
Seagull
(Randall Jarrell) Quote, Part Two
An Acmeist Oeuvre - Muse From the Mountain
(Helen Horton) Quote
After the Gester Who Never Was [Extract, Sara Boxer]
(Miroslav Holub) Quote
Oxygen, the Preliminary
(Juan Ramon Jimenez) Quote
Alibi
Score
Stalemate
Diary of a Tear - cutter
Lorca
Leverage
Virtual Tour, Aphrodite Revisited
One Hand Clapping
Batone and Boondocks
Dowsing
Betrayal
The Void
Niet   !!!
Communion
Hard-copy Department, Ukraine
What I Love Most
The Sorceress
Tipster

Space Odyssey
As The Night closes In
Structure
Scan
Hard Work
Bum Steer = The Science of It
We Who Came
Forecast
My Wings, My Fate
Karma-Ten
You Can't See the Sky For Concrete
Perfidity
Perchance…
Gruel
Thread
Schiller's 'Ode To Joy'
A Bolshevik Remembers
Super Moon
(Octavio Paz) Quote
Chequer

ABOUT THE AUTHOR

Stefanie Bennett has published over a dozen volumes of poetry, a libretto and a novel. She has tutored in The Institute of Modern Languages (James Cook University), acted as a publishing editor, and worked with Arts Action for Peace [No Nukes]. Of mixed heritage [Irish/Italian/ Paugussett-Shawnee] she was born in Townsville, Queensland, Australia in 1945.

Time-Line quotes:

Not many poets can get poems like these to come-off. I'm proud to own the collection. (Trevor Reeves)

A tough stance with sensitivity of feeling. The poems are highly provocative ... (Pam Law)

In this book one of the most original voices in Australia speaks thorugh the great spirits of poetry & they through her... (Judith Rodriguez)

With certainty the poems ring truer than most shining in the poetic filaments of this country. (Dimitris Tsaloumas)

Treating Bennett as a visionary poet the poems wear two hats: one posited as a present lyricism - & the second as a history 'Repel & Attract'. (Simon Eales)

The subject matter of the poems ranges widely, from the personal & introspective to the objectively political. Bennett is a skilled wordsmith & a hard thinker. (Michael Dugan)

PART ONE

Poetry remembers everything
that exhaustion strews
across a wasteland ...

ALISON CROGGON

OPUS FOR HEART AND STONE

My love, you are no more.
The soap-stone of youth
I borrowed from you
Sits opaque
And much too obviously
Beside the unused
Wrought-iron gate.

A tangled mess of wonga vine
And eucalypt
Brocade the slats - and
Cross the wide verandah.
An odd floor-board whines
To the wind's intrusion.
    I pace the uneven reckoning
Stepping out my years.

I've trodden on an ideal:
Done love's wish
A healthy blow
And survived to walk again.
Perhaps the cripple
Limps the cripple out ...
    I'm not game enough
To state anything beyond that.

I cannot judge your absence.
A fall of shadows
Rise to the noonday sun
And withdraw each evening.
Vivaldi's 'Four Seasons'
Reverberates through both
    The aged old dwelling
And this grey disciple.

I have grown resilient
With my sorrow.
A cape of holes I'll not cast off
Not matter how
The climate sways. I've become
My style. I accept that ache.
    The soap-stone of youth
    Is a found treasure
Beside the unused gate.

I talked that these poems
might speak
for what I couldn't say.

        DAN GERBER

WANTED

I want the name of the man who
Killed the stars.
I want his whereabouts, now, here and ...

>With my wooden leg
>With my lioness tooth
>With my subjective middle eye
>With my triple-barrel suicide.

I want the name of the man who
Killed the stars
Because
>He did it out of pity -

Because
>He's taught us what the dark brings forth -

Because
>At eventide my shadow pines another beggar
>Game enough to walk it.

MULTIPLICATION

What shall we do with the wounds
        We are imprisoning the thorns
What shall we do with the thorns
        We must save them for the final dictator
What shall we do with the final dictator
        We will make of him a puppet-master
What shall we do with the puppet-master
        We'll tell him how beautiful he is
What shall we do with beauty like this
        We can teach how reflections lie
What shall we do with such reflection
        Ah! Bandage the product and shelve it
What shall we do with the shelved product
        ... Just feed it to the thorns

As they multiply. Multiply.

DON'T CRY MY CHILDREN

They scold you for being
Too big for your boots.
For back-chatting,
For singing in quiet places,
For feeding the animals,
For questioning the damnation
Of some; the elation
Of others. They question
The questioning. You must
Not cry, my children!
It happens because it happens.

Soon you'll learn to laugh
In all the right quarters.
Soon, you'll learn to lie
With the best of them.
Soon, the answers will be
Covered by a bill-of-sale
You'll slip into comfortably.
The humans of this world
Clothe and cord their existence
In a way that costs the very
Earth, but not one red cent.

And, as for the odd one of you,
They can't take a chance on
The odds of a chance. The usual
Is dangerous. A close watch is kept.
They scold with laws fit
Only for the breaking. There's
The locking up, the throwing away
Of keys - and a thing called personality.
You wouldn't want to be
One of the oddities left crying?
Whatever you do, do not make the mistake
       Of answering me.

A GENERAL TRUTH

The value of time
Made tender
Is when
Two Sensei
Almond
Flowers are
Touched
With rain ...

HEARTS THAT DIE YOUNG

I clutched the vision
Of the magnolia
Fine as pollen -
The coloured halo
Of your hair.

Some hearts die young
Without wilt or piety.
These are the ones
- Master dulcissima,
I offer you now.

And this you'd known all along.
You took me walking
As a child, and through
Child eyes you pointed
To the Imera's silken flowing.

Ever young, forever there…
You said. And as I balanced
Blood oranges
By the seller's cart
And asked the whereabouts

Of day-stars and hermetic charts
Your smile fell upon
The Madonie peaks:
Each answer the same. There was
No failed mystery in your language.

And now I clutch at visions; I've work
To do. Sometimes with
Arrows that pierce
Heart and paper. Sometimes with
Rivers seeping, changing course.

But memory, you remind me,
Is landscape enough;
Scars - mended lines of living.
I raise mid-aged eyes
And the street of clouds

Rests on a field of white magnolias
- Ever there. Your final
Word… Mater dulcissima.
It must be so!
Fine as pollen, as haloed hair.

THE CAIRN

Refusing to float
They'll skip
Cross water
And dune

…This pyramid
Family.
First
Of the line - .

CUTTING THE CHAFF

Another pamphleteer's excommunicated -
Lampooned witless
Without repose.
Eyes on the shamrock,
Heart compounding
Beneath the iron button-hole.

I am a tulip detonates
Amid the heather,
Gnome to the word vice -
Night-watchman of
The class that rules. Ah! Christ,
He said as much when he called

On my sixteenth birth-date.
Borstal will maim
You saint Judas-Kiss - and I,
I will allow the legend tried
Continuance. You'll fall
Twice to my name!

Through the bottle-glass
Three decades
In the rousing,
There's talk of revival…
More defamation. Now -

They're shooting
The movie... Brendan!
How passe.
Why not rearrange the wake -
The candle lit
        Both ways;
That's apt respite.

WINGS

...What shall
I bring?
What should
I bring?
My hands
Are corned
But non the less
Empty.

My shoes?
They're worn.
My cloak
Scares
The scare-crow.
The handkerchief!
It's the collection
Of sodden weeping.

What must I bring you:
You who
Have everything
But
The herb
Of my
Epic
Father.

JOURNAL ENTRY

It's no illusion:
That Pavarotti
Finch
    Whistles
While she works
    Beside
An ochre
And red
Backdrop
    One
Shy octave
At a time.

MT. ETNA AND HORSES OF THE MOON: -
A song for the azure cameo

Now, finally, I want to carry the clear corn
Resurrected in my grandmother's veil.
I want to place the selenium where
It must sustain the object
Of this most cautious of customs
- Retain forever the bread host's transmutation.

Smoke is rising from the chimney. I will,
Bounteous mother, treat our guests
To a wake of your finery. Figs,
                        I have gathered -
Tomatoes - and crushed almonds!
Sweet yellow wine is to be shared with
The herdsman's son, the carabinieri , and those

From the grotto. Not wastrel nor saint
Should forget how you sang
And nurtured here. Concordantly,
The eyelids will be covered by the palms
Of your confettied hospice; crickets hum
In nearby thickets. At yuletide

I'll toss the sachet of camomile into
The lava's compendium then lay down
                      With the corn,
                      With the veil.

I COULD NOT TELL YOU [for Anna-Maria, aged 7]

You ask so many questions
I have to run, or hide
To keep up with you ...

How often do
The great ones pass?
Is music
The only true language?
How come the raven
Has blue and gold wings
In certain light?
Can a pebble
Remember its origins?

Atlantis reflects itself
In your eyes.
Long-ago prophets
Lend you their dreams;
Their dying symbols.
And the witching hours
Send you
Spice boxes and jade madonnas,
And moon beam-candy
In the shape of stars.
- You are
The sad harlequin
Of the world's estate.

Your love is
Out of time and place.
Yesterday, I found you
Talking , talking to
A new-found
Black rose.
Its thorns, they
Turned silver.
The leaves
- A softening red.

With your
Invincible angel
As my witness
I should have told you
The rose
Was dead; irreversibly dead.

I could not. I could
Not bring myself
To tell you that.

RESTITUTION

The town-hall clock
Has
Dropped
Its
Hands -

It has a habit
Of doing that.

Always.
But always,
Repair-men
Mend
Defeatists.

HEART

There is a room where a street hangs.
There is
      A street.
      A room
      Hung
      Sideways.

The walls of the room where
      The street hangs
& where the street has hung
      The room whose walls
        Are also sideways:
          Who has
          Never
          Entered!

AFTER 'OF GODS AND OLIVES'

Amid the babel of brandishing tongues
And your eaglet summer, Pritish Nandy -
The rickshaw wavers down Dhakura Bylane
To the last gaslamp's illicit nightshift...

   This is the season
                Of the black wall-flower,
   A gazelle trail
                Lined with gnarled hags.
   And you - Calcutta hawker,
                Accrue that oncoming exile
  -Your chest full of bullets, poems
                Lodged beyond the third eye.

Amid the babel of the savage quarter shade,
The monkey nuts and jade, Pritish Nandy -
A handcart is steered by tame leopards
To the gilded Supreme Court of Delhi.

   Still, the jaws of land
                Are seeking a cure...
   The broken harp hangs
                Askance in the share-market.
   Water rots in that
                Scented well, and tampaka tree
   And betel leaf shrivel
               To a worker's hands.

Amid the babel of lepers and king snakes
You wreathe to the tabla beat, Pritish Nandy -
Songs of the slayer; the brothel keeper;
Amendments to the ultimate order...the Gita!

   Now, what will sugar
                The most bereaved of fears?
  ... Prisoners of conscience
                From Sri Sri to Samar Sen?
  Not the Brahmin. The Shiekh.
                Sired opiate anti-Gods -
  Nor those who pass
                Auspicious lotus trays around.

Amid the babel of accusers and time's mallet
You unstitch the National lip, Pritish Nandy -
A threadbare sun warns of the danger - but you stride
Out of the dust, the chains

                In this interim:

Your torn robe unquestionably - burning.

ATHENA REGRETS

The mortal stars up there
    Seem to be
    Taking
    A beating.

Excuse the presumption.
    Attune the ear:
    Come
    Closer.

NOW AND THEN

Those were the times, Nigel.
Bohemia at its god-forsaken best.
Chinese tea and gin chasers
Down by the quay. We put the world
To order with a chant and a buddhist-bell.

Those were the days. Sundays stoked
With Robert wanting realism and surrealism
All at once. And us, swallowing the lot
In the shallow rooms off Forsyth Street where
Dylan was king and Baez his queen.

We'd perfected the art of buffoonery.
Pete had an almost perfect
Love affair with a third-hand printing press.
Carol spoke of dropping-in on Lesbos, while
Vicki made Nepal her marked Nirvana.

We dreamed our infantile dreams.
Crusaders of poets would rise up and
Swat the mote from the earth's eye.
Clearly, we saw then in sanctuary
What sets the mind to sobbing now.

Was it enough? To play at being toughs?
The sacrificial years swept us down and under
A carpet of tutelary-exempt tomorrows.
You became a lay-preacher. The others?
I couldn't hazard a guess. And I? I go on

Marking time. Occasionally word knitting
A new bullet-proof... vest.

[The Poets:
        Nigel Roberts
        Carol Novack
        Vicki Viidikas
         Robert Adamson
        Pete = Pi O

MINIATURE

As Lady Day
Begins
To fade,
The yellow
Bird
Voices freedom.

In the blink
Of an eye
      - Working
Over-time -,
He holds up
The sky

… And its Saviour.

FOR ALL NUCLEAR SCIENTISTS:
The Killing & The Telling

Last night 'Terror' died.
It died, not as it had
Lived in its own black death
- But with the soft glow
Of a green light about it.

I was cruel. I was kind...
I took from it the aches
And anguish of a life spent
Battling the human elements.
I spelt trust as a 4 letter word.

Last night 'Terror' spoke. It spoke
In syllables as wide as the sky.
When faced with its own
Ghosted-in image
The din cannot be described...

And I - perhaps with a little
Too much of the Don Quixote
In me, wielding a rusty pen
Instead of a sword
Made the decision that

>We kill for all reasons.
>Some bad. Some good.
>And some out of pity.

I erased 'Terror' from the vocabulary
- As if time's compass had not ever
Met this wretched one.
I do not know if the killing

Will, in turn, inturn me. There
Was a green light
Blazing about it.
Possibly that indicated
A pardon.

THE HURT

...Way out west
Where
The prickly-pear
Grows
    The salty
    Sun
Sits smack
    Bang
In the middle
    Of the road.

TOWER

Fetch me a line, one that
Won't prop up the nation.

Moon, toss back the dog,
It's given you cataplexy.

Be damned you horn-locking demons
Masquerading culture.

Taser the body. The body
You're hoping to save.

Lend that wit, sociology. The wit
Festering in the memory-bank zoo.

Just take yourselves off to bed.
Don't question what I'm about to do
            With your tools…

By morning you'll inherit
The labours you crave.

MEMENTO...THE MOUNTAIN OF SUNS

> "Before the fat
> one slims,
> the slim one
> dies."
>
> (Armenia Proverb)

You are...
        Still living in insurgency
              Sabbath lands -
The graticule
        Magnetizes
              That Parthian dynasty.
And the Arsacids*
        Once stoned with
              The morphology of age
Rise, inexorably again,
        To the old
              Humanistic order.*

The blacksmith's lame
        Enough - he walks
              His orthopaedic curse.
The ferryman's
        Witnessing another pre-dawned
              Cult of the dead.
Women, children;
        Toss their loaded
              Dream-scream dice as
Colchis trembles*
        Its blue acetylene ray
              To the throb of a quartz lamp.

I wear the rose monocle
>> Of reportage;
>>>> Add my own salamandering:
Stark yellow…! Black…!
>>> My fingerprints smudged, denailed
>>>> By muscovite wine.
No. Not even ascetic heroism
>>> Can condone
>>>> A one eyed troika mongering*
While all and sundry
>>> Wear the branded
>>>> Goat-skin lead-boot and cap.

There's three copecks worth
>>> Of sound
>>>> Forbidden your lips,
Enough to purchase
>>> The ingredients
>>>> For cabbage and mutton soup -
But not the ballad
>>> Of the ruins
>>>> In near forgotten Zvartnots*
… Or the malachite
>>> Precision unearthed
>>>> Within those Pushkin stanzas.
Here, at this moment
>>> Most copious, I glimpse
>>>> The peninsula of Sevan*
Where stonemasons
>>> Dug furiously
>>>> Their foundations so that

A veritable lighthouse
                Could be born
                              To shed gentle power
About the lands
                Affectionately known
                              As 'The Mountain of Suns.'

Who can forget, Armenia,
                Your Moscow accent?
                              Your frock-coat
Cut in Ottoman style?
                Your golden
                              Currency of cognac
Serving Japhetic philosophy*
                Born of
                              Noah's second sight?
The Hebrew prayer hands…
                Monk's tombs…
                              And grand sea serpents?

Meanwhile, the iron staircase
                Breathes a reticent
                              Mythological track…
How gravity dropped
                Three apples*
                              In bold parenthesis
To three esperanto
                Citizens seeking
                              Harmony of civility.
The first parable told
                The tale. The second
                              Was for the one who listened

And - the third, helix of the ear,
            It marked
                      The 'hermit' who understood.
Prototype provincialism, wry
            Ship of Peter,
                      Passes only nameless graves.
The bleeding thornbush
            Keeps vigil
                      To commissars caught and set agape
So that I... recorder-politico
            Cannot attempt redress
            Except in this:

            Abbi pieta - have mercy (inglese)
            Abbi pieta
            Abbi pieta.

Notes on the poem:

* Arsacids - ancient rulers
* Humanistic Order. Ref. is to Stalin's opposition
* Colchis - other name for Caucasus
* Troika - Russian 3 man administrative council
* Zvartnota - locals live by the sundial amid the ruins where a rose is inscribed in stone
* Japhetic - all pre-Indo-European languages belong to a racial group named after Noah's other son
* Three apples - ancient Armenian fairytale.

THE CURSE: HAMLET

I wear dark glasses.
I disgrace myself,
Admit the vision
We had
Was not new; and
If I am
Talking to myself
Yet again,
All the better
To keep me
On my toes - crouching.

These corners were not made
So that light
Could reach easily.
Here we learn
By touching
The silences.

THE DEVINE FEM

I've played down my stock of years
And kept the improvisation
For myself:

I designed the first heresiarch…

Mother to stone, feathering atmosphere,
My children hung as pendants
- The genetics of all.

I set the showground going.

The Muse had something to do with it.
The torch-swallower. The giantess
Of 'o' - and the gale that followed.

The tongue! It won't cease there.

FOLLOWING THE BALLAD 'GORBANEVSKAYA'

Imprisonment is never sweet. Natalya...
In or out of the garbage pail.

And - Clutter's affluence finds its keeper,
Chisel blue, solid as an amputable

Outlook; wholesome: the ensnarement drawn
On the first official day of spring.

- * -

Salaam -: you've run that race of numbers
Fleeced from the capitulated crypt.

The agent promises a secured apartment,
Hoar-frost at your beck and call

To illustrate those wolverine stuttered lines
Placed upon the page; digital -

- * -

A mummy's tomb. Graphiting in the dour details
As must be your custom,

Leaving party schisms in rags, you've realtered
The thaw.

Ah! Peeking through sanity's lattice, comes
The chuckling,
        "Balance yourselves..."

- * -

We try. Tenacity is not our forum. You pay
For this. You pay.

THE BRIEF

Sometimes, all the moon
Wants
Is to
Let down her hair
Into
The 'river
Of time' -.

SCOPE AND VALIDATION

All too quickly it vanishes. Take
The emotions,
Slide rules you vacate
With a permanency.

Love, you've not escaped.
You subsist. The soul
Merely reaffronts
In some other area. This

I remind myself unravelling
The blind over
My bare pain.
Still wilderness crowds on in.

GENEVA'S SWEET TWEETS

The talks that Absolve
Peace from any
Wrongdoing
Are underway -.

Touch
     Friendly-,
Cool
     To look at -,
Sobering
     To hold -,
Non-
     Negotiable -,

Cunningly
     Dyed-in
     The-wool
     'Cost
     Effective'
     In the here

     And…

IRIS ORACLE

The dirty linen's tumbled after
That last cursed war:
My crest fallen uncle can't come back.

I've trekked from the shores of
San Remo, past cathedrals
That reek of christian pitying...

To Valenza - where thirteen shrews
Wail in their eventide black
               Beneath seven stars
Forming the shape of the plough

To find one stone commemorates you
Giuseppe, partisan shot
By Germans and provisionals of Italian militia.

'And only my own kind will kill me' - *
Sang a brother
Facing another diabolical accord.

Surely this is where grief spins
It's curtain calling
               Among the fur trees;
The ritual of diametrical deceit.

Who's fallen? Never our national astronomer
Nor the ragged pennant
Restored along with the invaders.

I taste the bitterness of sulphur
No scythe
Can cut clean

- And we begin to curse together.
We who've unbridled the blood lore
Still holding Valhalla proud.

The italicised line is from * Osip Mandelstam

EARTH, WIND, FIRE

Do not touch me
Unless the knife
Is deep;
I cannot risk
Mere surface.

Never face me unless
Prepared
To take
My place
And continue
Taking.

Though all routes be
No more than
The goat's domain;
I'll see you there.
You'll know me.

HOME GROWN

The Dust Devil family
Spins
    Like a top,
Kicks
    Like a mule
And won't
    Ever forsake
    The past
    For last.

GUEST

You arrive wearing your fatigue like a uniform.
Your face pale, the texture of wax.
Your feet, Sir, so swollen; the leggings
Won't give. The tongue chafed thus it lodges
Back, pinned to the mouth's roof.

I won't question... that is, I won't ask
Who you are, or how long you'll stay.
My study is yours. Yes! By all means make
Use of the lamp. Also I've filled
The pen with ink. Do you request a blank tablet?

Of course this visit is confidential. I'll not
So much as offer a description. We're, all of us,
Masters and mules of disguise.

                                  You've arrived
Wearing your fatigue like a uniform.
The uniform - I reflect,
Has stood you well.
Now, what about
The beads, the spires...

BAGGAGE

I would like to remind
My dissenters

That often
The wrong key

In a worn lock
Will bring

The house
Down.

PASSAGE - MOSCOW 1915

"I know the truth - give up all other truths!
No need for people anywhere on earth to struggle."

Marina Tsvetayeva

I've not destroyed myself although
They said I would.
I've run my race, but never crookedly.
The diversions, on occasion, were necessary.

And, I've not measured fate. Lady luck
Had other plans.
Familiarity, fame - it's the same forgery
When you get down on all fours to look at it.

As for that plasmic boy, the one
Who deals out icons
And the wearing lands of the senses,
I read him as best I could.

We live separately. He, in his fine house
Scattered with bronze eagles,
Unicorn, and fire-wheels; I in my trench-coat,
Total... conventionless...

Mentor aside, the path was stony.
At every fork an ambush,
A reconciliation. Through the twin births
                                  Of opposites

I chose, always, what lay between.

After me comes
                Death in her doomed chariot.
I pause long enough
To kiss the living back to life.
I've learned destruction can be tender

...The process ongoing. The writing
Of it - seemingly natural.

MY GRANDFATHER'S VIOLIN

I can still hear my grandfather's violin.
He played as if he'd brought the whole
Of Italy with him…

He'd been a barrow-boy. he's sold fruit
And flowers outside the concert hall
Of Naples. He'd seen and known Caruso's last
Performance from the back row.

That concert cost him thirty barrow loads
And nine days of hard selling.
"I'd do it again," he'd say. "There are
Many apples but too few phenomenas."

I can still hear my grandfather's violin,
Hauntingly beautiful, drifting upwards
Like a prayer - like water trickling
About the flagstones in the back garden.

I see the old photographs hung near the stairwell.
The pin-stripe suit. The classic spats and hat
That lent 'a touch of class'. More than that:
His kind of tenacity shone on through.

He went as he'd lived. Glib and humorous.
His policy: things are what you make them.
He died comfortably off. It started
With a barrow full of fruit and flowers.

The violin? It held it all together.

SEAGULL

Devoid of abstraction
It settles like a hush
On the sagging jetty-rail.
Several aged fisherman
Make jokes to the tune
Of the first catch.

Probably, the morning
Is silver, with light rain
Misting the air.
And the largest of coins,
The sun, extends
Her sash about the land.

This morning, like any other
Must pass - and go on passing.
There is sadness. Wonder…
Try and hold it there.

PART TWO

'You can't break eggs without making an omelette
- that's what they tell the eggs'

RANDALL JARRELL

AN ACMEIST OEUVRE - Muse from the Mountain*

Wild fruits fall once again and time
Passes its orcharding. Leaves -
Their shape like hieroglyphs,
Make little of the future.

Where is 'the golden child' - the one
Who inherited my uppermost branches?
Who swayed and sang
As only innocence can? Perhaps

Now flown… and past recall! Past
The old vibrancy
Of a lover's gaze - stepped out - over
Grief's cleft and into another.

Utterances from a distant star:
They're shooting hearts
Into the frost of space.
It's no more than a rumour

… Something to
         Taunt emotion.
Lead it away
    From the self without self.

A horizontal shriek
         And gash
Streak across
      This last horizon. It is

Not my kin, my valuable! My love lies
Beneath the pressed foliage.
The brown earth.
The departing seasons.

*After 'Hope Abandoned' by Nardia Mandelstam

All the days of the world
are written in this sand.

HELEN HORTON

AFTER THE JESTER

WHO NEVER WAS

[Miroslav Holub]

Miroslav Holub (1923-1998) the Czech poet and immunologist was known for his ironic wit, his impatience with irrationality & his knife-like poetry. Shortly after the Prague Spring of 1968, Holub became a "non-person" & any mention of his work was forbidden. None of his poetry was published between 1970 & 1980. Seamus Heaney praised Holub as a poet who laid things bare. Holub's poetry, he wrote, is "Too compassionate to be vindictive, too skeptical to be entranced."

[Extract, Sara Boxer]

To prop the growing head
of Man
We seek
a backbone
that will stay
straight.

        Miroslav Holub

OXYGEN, THE PRELIMINARY

… Under a zeppelin cloud
On the corner of
The 'City of No Name',
The backgammon baker
- Who irradiated
Our first
Black Forest cake -,
(I.e. 'Day Duty 1958')
Didn't believe
In empires of sand,

The likelihood
Of Jean-Paul *
Returned as
A shoe-lace salesman, or
Trans-Baverian
Weevils frolicking
Throughout
The flour…

A practising practical
"Non-person", he
Did accommodate
Intrinsic mottoes
And their
Entangled surrounds
- Illustriously
Clichéd -;

To bark at a star
Spiked
With mercy -,

To tin-horn
          One's peers,
Generally
Speaking -,

And, when truncheoned
Between
Parallels

To deconstruct
The image.
So -!

Please note, Holub
How this
Post-haste
Sequence
Just is -,
Has no dissident
Entrance fee
- And alas,

No sound.

[* Jean-Paul Sartre]

Good-bye, you who are walking
without turning your head…

JUAN RAMON JIMENEZ

ALIBI

What simplicity…
The goddess is.
What simplicity:
Buddha too.

The equation:
Both exist,
Make one
Of the mould.

Who is there
    To be fooled!
Who thought up
    The disguise!

SCORE

On the night train
Heading homeward
The painted lady
Toyed her thoughts,
The guardsman,
               Nervous,
A firefly,
Punched tickets
Waist-deep in shadow
That the widower
Cast about
His new pink
Impressionable son.

Just this, on the night
Train heading
Homeward.

STALEMATE

Combat is
Not
Always
Enough.

(Be Seated!)

This is what
The Aliens
Termed
Resistance.

(Be Seated!)

I do
My
Best.
I do…

DIARY OF A TEAR-CUTTER

An image lived inside a sphere
Of the tear-cutter.
Her profession taught
This could not be so
Since image stands
Alone as image.

   Then I am quite mad,
   She sang. I believe
   In the micro-dot Magus
   And tears spearing
   All tongues
   Within the bed-clothes.

Besides, the tear, oblique
To science, will not
Dissolve in water;
Nor will it suffocate
Beneath the lands…

   I've seen it melt
   The most hardened diamond
   (She moaned)
   And exploded when told
   How useless it is.

Hand over hand equals the tear
Which is the image
Grossly misconstrued.
I must,
    She pledged,
Commence a school
Founded on failure
  That any tear-image
  Can pay homage to.

LORCA

Not even the dream hand
Un-knots you. I stretched it out
Never to placate you but
Take the wanton aback.

In your blind state... blind
Of a differing kind
I fingered nose, eyes, mouth
- And the ear's sounding tribunal.

Your heart I felt. I wanted
Its telling above others.
The roar it gave forth - worse
Than any air-raid. The manning of guns.

I surmised the pulse of your being
Should be aligned with hollyhocks.
I surmised
       A free flighted bird.
I surmised
       Storm clouds parted -

But there, on your brow
Something painted
A peal of bells
Where your mind struck five times

Not hours spent - never the dream hand -
Neither my grace or its own
Beguiled wretchedness could impede
What was or isn't there.

LEVERAGE

Scissors know our healing does not
Come from books:

Does as
    The wind does
Does arch
    As the hand raised over-long
Does concentrate
    On every pose
Does cheat
    For the sake of comfort
Does define
    Both prong and tail
Does the
    Daylights from the living
Does assign
    A dearth stance
Of which we are too familiar - cut
    From the background
What scrap is to the stockpiling.

VIRTUAL TOUR, APHRODITE REVISITED

My body was on show. The people
Paid, and handsomely,
To see this body,
To tell lovers, children,
Wives, how
Alive and well
The 'mad madam' stood

… Of the trick she pulled,
Screwing and unscrewing
Her head from
Sunrise to sunset. The 'Death
Of Poetry' the caption read.
Try it sometime.
Alone. With a friend.

ONE HAND CLAPPING

Feel in colour. The destruction of voice
Is mild green, terminable.

Easy on the eyes; paint ash or lilac
As if they could not see.

Tri-colour the body from the head's pivot
To the realm of the drum-roll's sad soul

And tread by the throats of flowers.
The scents of morning. The air's

Dominion. Feel. Feel in colour! Where
The black hatband

Has nowhere to rest… and the white glove
Claps farewell…

BATONS AND BOONDOCKS

Why am I dreaming
Of young grenadiers
And the night's
Mawkish militancy -

A carnation, unwieldy bowed,
Receding
In a row
Of saltbush

That didn't turn
True-blue
      But peaked,
Lacquered
Thin as

An oppressed mortal's
Herring-
Bone
Shroud and

The stoked-up
Ricochet
Of attrition
On the run!

Must be Faust's off-siders
Doing the rounds.

DOWSING

One blade of grass
Will weather all seasons,
Trawl a spider's thread
Through the chimera wound
As D-day approaches.

Listen. Do you hear the crib
Shrieking empty
In the holster
Of the wind? That's
Convergence!

One blade of grass -
              Flexible,
Covets the key
To antiquity
And stays
The discus thrower.

Not of this era, passers-by mistake
Transparency for rubble.

BETRAYAL

Clocks. There are too many clocks.
There are too few many homo sapiens
Who do not aspire to clocks.

See the mouse run. It is the machinist.
It attends the clock arms.
In any event it'll corrode with the battery.

Attention! The clock has gone sour.
She spat out her spring. Disrupted
The schedule of trains and the iron bird also.

What to do when the clock revolts?
When the clock family, a billion-fold,
Climb down from the wall and leave it…

We know what we'll do. A concentration camp
For clocks in peace-time's a bore.
Say, what else is our military for?

THE VOID

If my hand hadn't trembled so
I'd not have
Let go of the moon.
Pluto and Mars
Wouldn't be
Warring it up
And I, I needn't be left
To conquer
One dismal room with
A fountain-pen,
Four gratuitous
Off-white walls - and
My head
      Aside
As paper-weight.

NIET!!!

No -, we don't play
Spin-the-bottle
Any more.

Instead we watch
The day
Explode

Its chalice
Of electrodes
Rippling

The caustic air,
And a canal
That won't

Stop weeping.

COMMUNION

The truth of the matter?
I grow tired
Of the vision grotesque,
Angels stuck
In trumpets and
A Dutch painter's *
Shifty counterpart...

Indeed, at my table, I have
Company serene.
The bust
Of Alexander Blok:
The pick of the litter.

* Hieronymus Bosch

HARD-COPY DEPARTMENT, UKRAINE

What must word-play
Do with
A subject
The doesn't exist!

Revisit the flaw
Through
      'The Looking-Glass War'
Says Alice.

WHAT I LOVE MOST

Pure white stones haphazard as my mantelpiece.
Bees of no order enticing the ear.
Smouldering sands, the cathedral of summer,
And multiple armed pine trees
                     Living out an invocation.
It's what I can't love
                 That bothers me the most...

For years I've set up my heart on trial.
We cannot know exactly which way
Our dust bowl confesses,
Or what is outright affrontery.

Loving some is not enough.
Loving all is the trickery acquired
To live non-dangerously
In a world busy chasing its tail.

I remember my beneficence now
And again. Gently I make way
Through the good. Reservedly
I snap the jaws
              Of evil as if
It were part
           Of the daily chore.

THE SORCERESS

Come to me under glass.
(I abstain.)
We won't bother, then,
With the monologue.
(Again, I abstain)
Where's the gain!
Once you've lost,
You've lost.

TIPSTER

On nights of the full moon
I batten
Down the hatch
For who knows what city-slickers
Will tally up to.

All and sundry's fumigated,
Especially the wicker chair
Belching collywobbles and
Covered in hoar frost
… The lair where

An enthused meteor squats
And resumes his Promethean
Shock-jock tale
Of devil's dust
Gone loco.

Beware of the pith and marrow,
He intones.
It's 'sucking eggs'
That make
Wise counsel.

SPACE ODYSSEY

Surrounded by
Grey days
You lose

When love's
Lost
In the wash.

AS THE NIGHT CLOSES IN

…Too large to enter an exit
The dwarf in polkadot coat-tails
Cries twixt squabbles of shade:

    It's always this way around twilight.

Under the fringe of reliability
Limps the prospector of lame things.
Call it whatever

    It's just some beggar seeking hunger.

Too small to reach a congregation
Amid elephants, the ant is lost
In the toss of innocence - Hell!

    It's only a mind against triggered matter.

STRUCTURE

It's not 'The Bracket
Creep'
I worry about,
But the shadow's
Eye for
An eye
Deceit
Of it -.

SCAN

Just as light dips its corona
My lodger - an echidna
By any other name -
Zigzags the curved terrace
To forage her banquet,
Leaving furrows
Between iris and sage.

Sighted, our eyes interlock.
I blink; make hexagrams
From antiquated toil,
Shout
      "Eureka..."
The Buddha's been
A long time
Coming.

HARD WORK

The last conversation
I had
With a fossil
Escapes me -.

It's either -, or
Neither -,
Of us
Being known

To the other
That
Counts as
A bit

Of a bother...

BUM STEER = The Science Of It

My poetry's made a friend of you. This
Need not have been so. Always
You have hammered,
'Write me! Paint me tan! Centre
On my worthiness!'

Ah!
    A wishbone
    For vanity.
    A jaw.
    A claw and
    A thousand score
    Blank pages.

I am homely. Poor and not
At all disreputable.

WE WHO CAME

We who came through the generations
        Emptied the pepper
        All over the dessert,
        Knifed arabic
        In the gravy,
        Dealt out spoons
        - The royal
        Flush of poker,
        Turned the wineglass
        Into paper-cups,
        Fed cheese and anchovy
        'Over there'
        To a mange-mimic connoisseur.
        Set the finger-bowl alight
        And quarrelled
        Words and sent
        Then packing
        Off to
        Another's serious luncheon…

The balloons we left intact.
Air. No-one's put a price on it.

FORECAST

There are specks of blood
On the freeway.
A dog's met death:
Met it head-on.
We allow some sort of pity.

There are specks of blood
Of a different kind;
A kind that can't be seen
When someone's ravaged a forest
And a eucalypt's become a black hole.

There are specks of blood, historic
Specks, left to be gloried at.
Zelda. Lorca. The common lovers,
Anthony and Cleopatra
And all the king's men.

There are specks and more specks
Upon your motherly aprons
America! Russia! Your
Off-spring grow weak
With your manic menopause.

There are specks of blood
On the lips of infinity.
Hell is on holiday.
Lucifer's taken his leave.
The gardenia's armed and dangerous.

MY WINGS, MY FATE

My misplaced pencil-sharpener,
How is it I'm to manage
The analogue without you…
Who beckoned you from
Your rightful place?
Was the act committed
While I was sleeping?
My head turned?
Did I simply neglect you
For too long?

Come back down! You don't
Belong in the heavens.
Reshaping the stars
Is my judgement.
Forgive me. Forgive me.

KARMA-TEN

It was what the cat foretold:
Straying happens
But once in a while.
No homing device
Was needed
To shout it back:
No rulings, no body-snatcher.

Of an accord best let be
Cats return to

    A cracked saucer,
    A sinking ship
    If that's what
    The tenth life
    Ordered.

YOU CAN'T SEE THE SKY FOR CONCRETE

...At times like these, I wish
The great slab
Of blue and
Horse's manes
In the wind to
Descend
Their science
To landscape
And sculpture out
A space for living:

The pigeon cowers
By monuments
    At times like these.

I pack my luggage
For something to do
    At times like these.

Drink un-afforded white-horse spirits:
Imagine Mayans in all levis
    Swishing by...
At times
Like these times.

PERFIDITY

Someone's perfected an Odyssey.
Someone's thrown the ball in the court.
Someone's lauded the catch
Watch him trembling.
Someone's imagining there'll be 'no pass'.

Someone's bodily coveting the ground.
Someone's got a hooter she can't blow
It's not half-time.
Someone's dreaming… 'I'm dreaming'.
Someone's convinced this is traitorous.

Someone's taking off an expensive suit.
Someone's emptying their pockets.
Someone's writing IOUs
And someone's
          Shell-shocked by ovation as
The bald planet ticks over into the grandstand.

PERCHANCE

The tortoise
Waits
For
The post
To shift
Of its own
Volition.

GRUEL

There's no need to substantiate
The highs and lows
That expediency delivers...

Like a spent post-card.

Revival of the Ancients.

An untitled sonatina - or

The licensee means-testing
A solitary snapdragon
Thrashing

In the shade's
Withered
Loop.

THREAD

That book by Aleksander Wat
Housed the stone echo
Of a rose-water fountain,
And the unrefined epithet
Of a tutelary sparrow:

As well, it held
The orchestrated
Drift of freedom-come
Where all is no more
Than a storm passed over...

In my back o' Bourke's back-pack's
Dusty pocket
I carry the wild call
Of dissident worlds
Torched bare

- One crow's peck away
From grandeur;
From despair.

SCHILLER'S 'ODE TO JOY'

The tribe is not lost...
Replacements will come,
You'll see.

The bloody axes
                Will come.
The sonic blowpipe
                Will come.
And later 'the book'
                Will come
Wheeling in
                Its missionaries.

            All will come -
As past becomes. Everything
Reserves some right to glory.

The tribe is not lost.
Its too human face
Has simply
            Fallen.

A BOLSHEVIK REMEMBERS

Rode it out for hours,
Delivered it
Piece by piece.
              That
Collage
Spoke my voyageur

Once blew
A daily
To bits.

SUPER MOON

She has been inside that phone-box
An hour or more, dripping red
Upon the receiver, sirening loss.
It must be bad news; her own.
I haven't read it
In the papers
And bill-boards bleed
'Nothing's new.'

She wipes her eyes
On an apron, forehead
Transferring
          To glass.

   … What news… Her news,
      That turns old women
      Into sieves!

…The burning tree quivers
surrounded now by night.
Talking to it I talk to you.

          OCTAVIO PAZ

CHEQUER

It wasn't perfect, we did not
Go down
In flames
Or fly
The cerebral kite
On shores
Less foreign.

Drifting, interfused
With twists
Of fallibility
And Gitanes
Tasting like
      Barometric
Corn-syrup, we

Read Ferlinghetti's
'City Lights',
Caught
The last bus
Back
To specifics
That didn't add up
And an ending that
Never was.

Thank goodness somebody thinks poems are forever. What you say of Tsvetayeva may as well apply to you.

                          Judith Wright

www.ingramcontent.com/pod-product-compliance
Lightning Source LLC
Chambersburg PA
CBHW031126080526
44587CB00011B/1123